MW01689092

GOD KNOWS BEST ABOUT STRESS

Biblical Reflections to Lift Up the Heart

Fun Nun®
Sister Mary Christelle Macaluso
RSM, OFN, PhD
web site: www.FUNNUN.com

Fun Nun® Books
College of Saint Mary
Omaha, Nebraska USA 68124-2377

Scripture quotations are taken from *The Living Bible* copyright ©1971. Used by permission of Tyndale House Publishers, Inc., Wheaton, Illinois 60189. All Rights Reserved.

Layout by Carol Sayers
Cover Design by Carol Sayers
Printed in the United States of America
by United Graphics Inc., Mattoon, IL

15 14 13 12 11 10 9 8 7 6 5 4 3 2 1

Copyright ©2000 by the Fun Nun®,
Sister M. Christelle Macaluso, RSM, OFN, PhD
Library of Congress
Catalog Card Number: 00-190679
ISBN: 0-9663462-2-X

All rights reserved. Printed in the United States of America. Contents and/or cover may not be reproduced in whole or in any form without the express written consent of the publisher.

Publisher: Fun Nun® Books
College of Saint Mary
Omaha, Nebraska USA 68124-2377
402-399-2474 FAX: 402-399-2686
E-Mail: funnun@csm.edu
Web Site: www.FUNNUN.com

DEDICATION

To all those who
are overstressed.

To all those who
are understressed.

To all those who
are looking
for a deeper
meaning in life.

To all those who
are looking for God.

To all those who
have found God.

ACKNOWLEDGMENTS

No book ever comes to completion without the involvement of many people. Surely this book is no exception. I am grateful to Carol Corey. From the very first day she shared my vision, encouraged me, and worked endlessly along the way. I'm in debt to Shirley Trout, author of ***Light Dances***, who shared her gifts with me in so many ways – especially her insights and her professional knowledge about writing books. I thank Carol Sayers for the layout and cover. I have my friend, Marcia Borello, to thank for the series title ***God Knows Best About...***, and the Sisters of Mercy who have always encouraged my endeavors. I appreciate the College of Saint Mary for all its support, and Polly Nimmer, Sister Dolores Preisinger, RSM, and Carol Corey for their editorial advice. Thanks to my family and friends who supported my goals and to any of you I may have forgotten.

ABOUT THE AUTHOR

The Fun Nun, Sister Mary Christelle Macaluso, RSM, OFN, PhD, is a full-time professional speaker and has been so since 1980. She teaches people how to live more joyfully and reduce their stress levels. She speaks nationally and internationally to business, health, education, government, religious, and social groups. The Fun Nun has been on many radio talk shows and has appeared on national television. She is a member of the National Speakers Association.

Before becoming a professional speaker, the Fun Nun taught for 16 years at College of Saint Mary in Omaha, Nebraska. Her educational background includes a BS from College of Saint Mary, a MS from the University of Notre Dame, and a PhD from the University of Nebraska.

God Knows Best About Stress is the second book in the Fun Nun's series, ***God Knows Best About...*** The first book of the series is ***God Knows Best About Joy***. Each book highlights Scripture passages that correspond with its theme. If you want more details about her forthcoming books, please contact her.

The Order of the Fun Nuns (OFN) founded by Sister has thousands of members. Members are encouraged to spread some joy each day in their own way. There is a membership card for you on the following page.

The Fun Nun® will make you laugh while you are learning! She speaks on topics related to humor, stress, and self-image. If you need to add some life and zest to your program, invite the Fun Nun®! Contact her by any of the following ways:

Phone: 402-399-2474
Fax: 402-399-2686
E-Mail: funnun@csm.edu
Web Site: www.FUNNUN.com
Address: College of Saint Mary
1901 S. 72nd St.
Omaha, NE USA 68124-2377

MEMBERSHIP CARD

ORDER OF
THE FUN NUNS (OFN)

OPEN TO ALL

A MERRY HEART DOES LIKE GOOD MEDICINE

PROVERBS 17:22

I,____,

SPREAD SOME JOY
EACH DAY IN MY OWN WAY.

FUN NUN®
SISTER M. CHRISTELLE MACALUSO, RSM, OFN, PhD
COLLEGE OF SAINT MARY
1901 S. 72ND ST., OMAHA, NE 68124-2377
402-399-2474, FAX: 402-399-2686
E-MAIL: funnun@csm.edu
WEB SITE: www.FUNNUN.com

INTRODUCTION

Books similar to this have taken quotes of famous persons or wise sayings and matched them with Bible verses. My books, ***God Knows Best About Stress*** and ***God Knows Best About Joy***, differ from these. I've taken a theme, selected biblical passages that represent this theme, and offered a personal reflection on them.

This is the second book of a series titled ***God Knows Best About...*** There are many passages in the Bible that show how stressful living was in Biblical times. The wisdom of the Bible gives answers on how to cope with stress.

I chose ***The Living Bible*** because the translation uses words and expressions that agree with common parlance.

My prayer is that you are helped to overcome stress in your life as you ponder the words in this book.

Fun Nun®
Sister Mary Christelle Macaluso,
RSM, OFN, PhD
College of Saint Mary
Omaha, Nebraska USA

GOD KNOWS BEST ABOUT STRESS

FUN NUN®

SISTER MARY CHRISTELLE MACALUSO
RSM, OFN, PhD

But they that wait upon the Lord shall renew their strength. They shall mount up with wings like eagles; they shall run and not be weary and not faint.

Isaiah 40:31

4/6/20

Stress zaps your strength. Your energy is finite and needs to be renewed. There is no greater source of strength than God.

It is senseless for you to work so hard from early morning until late at night, fearing you will starve to death; for God wants his loved ones to get their proper rest.

Psalm 127:2

Not enough time!
Not enough time!
This is modern society's
constant cry.
God wants you
to take time to
smell the roses.

So get rid of your feelings of hatred. Don't just pretend to be good! Be done with dishonesty and jealousy and talking about others behind their backs.

1 Peter 2:1

Sin is the greatest
stressor of all.
For stress reduction
follow the words
of Christ given
to the woman
caught in adultery,
"Go and sin no more"
(John 8:11).

Gentle words cause life and health; griping brings discouragement.

Proverbs 15:4

Are you a griper?
Do people want to
plug their ears in
your presence?
Speak kindly.
You will reduce
their stress levels
and yours!

Then Rebekah said to Isaac, "I'm sick and tired of these local girls. I'd rather die than see Jacob marry one of them."

Genesis 27:46

Remember how
you finished your
mother's statement
when she said,
"I'm sick," and
you said, "and tired."
Biblical moms
had stress.
Times don't
change much!

I am leaving you with a gift — peace of mind and heart! And the peace I give isn't fragile like the peace the world gives. So don't be troubled or afraid!

John 14:27

Ask for the
Lord's kind
of peace.
It ranks #1
in stress reduction.

These troubles and sufferings of ours are, after all, quite small and won't last very long. Yet this short time of distress will result in God's richest blessings upon us forever and ever!

2 Corinthians 4:17

Most of our stress comes from hassles and not major crises. Hassles act like termites that eat small bits of wood yet can bring down a mansion! List ten of your most bothersome hassles. Decide on a strategy to cope with each. Please include prayer.

Bend down and hear my prayer, O Lord, for I am deep in trouble.

Psalm 86:1

Remember how stressed you were when you experienced deep trouble? Your heart pounded, your breath was short, and every muscle was tense. You felt helpless. Did you call on the Lord to help you?

Don't worry about anything; instead, pray about everything; tell God your needs and don't forget to thank him for his answers. If you do this you will experience God's peace, which is far more wonderful than the human mind can understand...

Philippians 4:6-7

How much of
your day do you
spend worrying?
How much of
your day do you
spend praying?
Worry brings stress,
but prayer
brings peace.

... Shall we receive only pleasant things from the hand of God and never anything unpleasant?" So in all this Job said nothing wrong.

Job 2:10

Trials test your faith
and trust in God.
Pray for the
patience of Job.

How wonderful it is, how pleasant, when brothers live in harmony!

Psalm 133:1

This world lacks
harmony. Divorce
rates are up.
Crime is increasing.
There is religious strife.
Be an example
and live in harmony
with others.
You can start
a chain reaction!

Stop being mean, bad-tempered, and angry. Quarreling, harsh words, and dislike of others should have no place in your lives. Instead, be kind to each other, tenderhearted, forgiving one another, just as God has forgiven you because you belong to God.

Ephesians 4:31-32

Your actions can
cause stress
or give peace
and love.
You have a choice.
Remember, all
are your brothers
and sisters in Christ.

Jesus was tired from the long walk in the hot sun and sat wearily beside the well.

John 4:6

Jesus was God
and man. He felt
the stress of travel.
You are stressed
making plane
connections, getting
stuck in traffic,
having car problems.
Jesus stopped
for a drink of water.
In your travels take
some time to relax.

Lord, hear my prayer! Listen to my plea! Don't turn away from me in this time of distress. Bend down your ear and give me speedy answers.

Psalm 102:1-2

You would like
speedy answers
to all your prayers.
God doesn't always
answer at the snap
of your fingers.
He sees the bigger
picture. Do you try
to do likewise?

In all you do,
I want you to be free
from worry...

1 Corinthians 7:32

God wants you free
of worry in all things.
This demands of you
great trust in God.
If you can't trust Him,
what greater choice
do you have?
Think it over.

But Martha was the jittery type, and was worrying over the big dinner she was preparing. She came to Jesus and said, "Sir, doesn't it seem unfair to you that my sister just sits here while I do all the work? Tell her to come and help me."... "Martha, dear friend, you are so upset over all these details!"

Luke 10:40-42

So much stress in life
is caused by giving
too much attention
to the non-essentials.

Anxious hearts are very heavy but a word of encouragement does wonders!

Proverbs 12:25

Do you find it hard
to give a word
of encouragement
to one in need?
Do you feel awkward?
Can't find the
right words?
How about trying
a hug, a hand
on the shoulder,
a card, a flower...?
Let another know you
are there for support.

Don't quarrel with anyone. Be at peace with everyone, just as much as possible.

Romans 12:18

Why do you quarrel?
Is your pride
preventing you
from seeing the
other's viewpoint?
Seek peace
and lower your
stress level.

There is a strange thing happening here upon earth. Providence seems to treat some good men as though they were wicked, and some wicked men as though they were good. This is all very vexing and troublesome!

Ecclesiastes 8:14

Surely, you have
often thought the
same thing!
Yet, deep inside
you know God is
in control, and all
things work unto
good. Let your
faith ease your stress.

It is better to eat soup with someone you love than steak with someone you hate.

Proverbs 15:17

Are some of your social gatherings worth it? You "have" to be there instead of "wanting" to be there. Maybe you need to learn to say "No." How about taking an assertiveness training class?

So get rid of all that is wrong in your life, both inside and outside...

James 1:21

You can do it!
Ask God, and
He will give you
the grace to
change your life.
Get a fresh start!

O Lord, have mercy on me in my anguish. My eyes are red from weeping; my health is broken from sorrow. I am pining away with grief; my years are shortened, drained away because of sadness. My sins have sapped my strength; I stoop with sorrow and with shame.

Psalm 31:9-10

King David was
stressed when
he wrote this.
Yet, what a powerful
prayer came from
his heart. It is a
prayer best put
to memory.
"O Lord, have
mercy on me in
my anguish."

The judge ignored her for awhile, but eventually she got on his nerves. "I fear neither God nor man," he said to himself, "but this woman bothers me. I'm going to see she gets justice, for she is wearing me out with her constant coming!"

Luke 18:4-5

Christ told this story
so you would
understand the
need to pray
and never give up.
However, remember
a "No" is also an
answer to prayer.

But I'm not the person for a job like that!" Moses exclaimed. Then God told him, "I will certainly be with you..."

Exodus 3:11-12

Fear is a
great stressor.
It makes you
feel inadequate.
Place your
confidence in God.
He is there
walking with you.

...No temptation is irresistible. You can trust God to keep the temptation from becoming so strong that you can't stand up against it, for he has promised this and will do what he says...

1 Corinthians 10:13

Have you ever
used the excuse
"The devil made
me do it!"?
You did not seek
strength in prayer.
God is with you
24 hours a day.
Don't ever
forget that!

A relaxed attitude lengthens a man's life; jealousy rots it away.

Proverbs 14:30

Want to live
a longer life?
Learn to cope
with stress. You need
to relax from tension
built up each day.
Evil thoughts may
be as damaging as
bacteria and viruses.

So don't criticize each other any more...

Romans 14:13

Are you a perpetual
or part-time critic
of others? Criticism
is so destructive
of others.
So stop it!

Let not your heart be troubled. You are trusting God, now trust in me.

John 14:1

Jesus is the
Son of God.
He is the "I am."
In *Genesis 1:26*
God said,
"Let us make" not
"Let me make."
There are three
persons in one God.
So you can place
your trust in Jesus.

*Listen closely
to my prayer, O God.
Hear my urgent cry.
I will call to you
whenever trouble strikes
and you will help me.*

Psalm 86:6-7

Don't just
call on God
in troubled times.
Call Him also in
good times.
He appreciates
words as
"Thank You,"
"I love You,"
"All praise be Yours."

And besides, what's the use of worrying? What good does it do? Will it add a single day to your life? Of course not! And if worry can't even do such little things as that, what's the use of worrying over bigger things?

Luke 12:25

Little worries!
Medium worries!
Big worries!
All of these take
away your time
and energy.
A big investment,
with no reward.

But Moses said, "They won't believe me! They won't do what I tell them to. They'll say, 'Jehovah never appeared to you!' "

Exodus 4:1

Do people's
expectations
affect you?
Do you need
their approval on
how you act,
how you talk,
how you think,
how you dress?
Do you really
need this stress?

A short-tempered man must bear his own penalty; you can't do much to help him. If you try once you must try a dozen times!

Proverbs 19:19

Research shows
that anger
and hostility
negatively affect
your health.
Learn to
control your temper
for a longer life.

... Live in harmony and peace...

2 Corinthians 13:11

It is irrational not
to live in harmony
and peace.
Yet, the world
chooses otherwise.
Even if all outside
of you is in turmoil,
you can seek
interior calmness
through prayer
and meditation.

But all who humble themselves before the Lord shall be given every blessing and shall have a wonderful peace.

Psalm 37:11

Your pride constantly
fights against humility.
God is infinite,
and you are finite.
You need His help.
Just ask.
Open your heart.

It is hard to stop a quarrel once it starts, so don't let it begin.

Proverbs 17:14

An ounce of
prevention
is worth a pound
of relaxation.
Conserve your
energy for
worthwhile activities.
Don't use
your energy for
actions that cause
needless stress.

The Lord is my light and my salvation; whom shall I fear?

Psalm 27:1

Rational fear
allows for sensible
precautions.
In all cases, let
God be your guide.

...Any kingdom filled with civil war is doomed, so is a home filled with argument and strife.

Luke 11:17

What ever happened
to "Home Sweet
Home"? Where is
the love holding
the family together?
Learn to forgive.
Start saying,
"I love you"
and mean it.

Only the Lord knows! He searches all hearts and examines deepest motives so he can give to each person his right reward according to his deeds – how he has lived.

Jeremiah 17:10

God notices
even the smallest
act of charity.
God works
through you.
Bring happiness
to others.
Pass on His love.

A rebel shouts in anger; a wise man holds his temper in and cools it.

Proverbs 29:11

Ask for the gift of wisdom. With it you will make choices that spare you from stressful situations.

. . . Watch out that no bitterness takes root among you, for as it springs up it causes deep trouble, hurting many in their spiritual lives.

Hebrews 12:15

Help others on
their spiritual journey
to God. Never be
to them a
stumbling block.
The less loving
you are, the farther
you drift from God
who is infinite love.

There was a time I wouldn't admit what a sinner I was. But my dishonesty made me miserable and filled my days with frustration.

Psalm 32:3

You are a sinner.
Lack of repentance
causes stress.
God is loving
and forgiving.
Ask God
to forgive you.
Then forget
about the past
and start anew!

...Everything is utterly weary and tiresome. No matter how much we see, we are never satisfied; no matter how much we hear, we are not content.

Ecclesiastes 1:8

The things of
this earth will
never satisfy you.
God is what
your heart desires.
Only by being with
God in heaven
will you be fulfilled.
Live a good life.
Your reward is great.

But Jesus didn't trust them, for he knew mankind to the core. No one needed to tell him how changeable human nature is!

John 2:24-25

Human nature
has not changed
over the years.
However, Christ's
coming has
given you the
power to change.
Turn your life to Him.

He will not break the bruised reed, nor quench the dimly burning flame. He will encourage the fainthearted, those tempted to despair. He will see full justice given to all who have been wronged.

Isaiah 42:3

Although the
Lord is just,
He is also gentle.
God cares
tenderly for you.
Invite Him to
renew your spirit.

It is better to be slow-tempered than famous; it is better to have self-control than to control an army.

Proverbs 16:32

In fact, controlling
an army might even
be easier than
self-control! Your
desires are great.
So many desires are
for temporal things.
Far better the desire
for holiness and
doing the will of God.

They load you with impossible demands that they themselves don't even try to keep.

Matthew 23:4

Do you put burdens
on others that you
would not carry?
If you manage
others, do you
make their jobs a
heaven or a hell?
In your family do
you rule with an
iron fist or
a heart of love?

I cannot sleep until you act. I am too distressed even to pray!

Psalm 77:4

Prayer is not
always easy.
You are burdened
with the concerns
and problems
of the day.
Tell God
you are too
troubled to pray,
and that is
your prayer!

Moses said to the Lord... "I can't carry this nation by myself! The load is far too heavy! If you are going to treat me like this, please kill me right now; it will be a kindness! Let me out of this impossible situation!"

Numbers 11:11,14-15

Don't you love this
prayer of Moses?
Perhaps you've
felt just like
him at times.
Follow Moses'
example and
cry out to God
about how you feel.

Hear my cry, for I am very low. Rescue me from my persecutors, for they are too strong for me.

Psalm 142:6

You have low days.
You have high days.
However, don't forget
to pray for strength
on the low ones and
to thank God for
the high ones!

A soft answer turns away wrath, but harsh words cause quarrels.

Proverbs 15:1

You have a choice
about how you
respond to others.
Sometimes you need
to bite your tongue
and stop the
urge to be harsh.
Conquer wrath
with gentleness.

...Be patient in trouble, and prayerful always.

Romans 12:12

You have your rights and feel they must be heard – now! Before you lash out, take a deep breath, calm yourself, and ask God to help you. Problems can be solved peacefully.

What is wrong cannot be righted; it is water over the dam, and there is no use thinking of what might have been.

Ecclesiastes 1:15

You cannot go back in time. Look at your thoughts. "I should have said this." "I should have done that." It's over and too late for "shoulds." "Should" is a high stress word. Try to do better the next time and learn from the experience.

First go and prove by the way you live that you really have repented...

Luke 3:8

Actions speak
louder than words.
Words are easy.
Ask God for the
strength to show
by your actions
that you
have changed.

Come quickly, Lord, and answer me, for my depression deepens; don't turn away from me or I shall die.

Psalm 143:7

You may turn
away from God,
but He will never
turn away from you.

You're going to wear yourself out — and if you do, what will happen to the people? Moses, this job is too heavy a burden for you to handle all by yourself."

Exodus 18:18

Are you too proud
to ask for help
when you need it?
Do you feel you
are Superman or
Wonder Woman?
Learn to delegate.
Remember the
world will go on
without you even if
you think otherwise!

I cling to your commands and follow them as closely as I can. Lord, don't let me make a mess of things.

Psalm 119:31

God gave you the
Ten Commandments.
These ten can
be condensed into
love of God,
neighbor, and yourself.
God wants you to
follow His directions.
He knows you are
imperfect and will
mess up periodically.
God is ready
to forgive.
Are you ready to ask
for forgiveness?

Can anyone hide from me? Am I not everywhere in all of heaven and earth?

Jeremiah 23:24

Everywhere includes
inside of you.
You are God's temple.
He loves you, and
you can never
escape His love.
He is the
"Hound of Heaven."

The good man does not escape all troubles — he has them too. But the Lord helps him in each and every way.

Psalm 34:19

Being good doesn't mean life will be easy for you. An athlete must train and suffer aches and pains for the glory of winning. In the race to heaven, all have the potential of winning. Are you ready for the sacrifice needed?

When the Lord God saw the extent of human wickedness, and that the trend and direction of men's lives were only toward evil, he was sorry he had made them. It broke his heart.

Genesis 6:5-6

Sin is the cause of all evil. If humans would stop sinning and start loving, our world would change. The poor would be fed, clothed, and sheltered. The sick would be comforted. Criminals would repent. Governments would be just. The uneducated would be schooled. Do your part to add some heaven on earth.

Immediately the Holy Spirit urged Jesus into the desert. There, for forty days, alone except for desert animals, he was subjected to Satan's temptations to sin.

Mark 1:12-13

The devil is strong,
but God is stronger.
Christ was tempted,
but He did not sin.
You will have many
temptations in life
because the devil
wants to drag you
away from God.
Say often the
"Our Father."
Ask God to deliver
you from evil.

O my soul, why be so gloomy and discouraged? Trust in God! I shall again praise him for his wondrous help; he will make me smile again, for he is my God!

Psalm 43:5

How often do you
walk around with
a long face?
Things are just
not going right.
Pressure! Pressure!
Pressure!
Need help? Well,
you know whom
to ask and trust.
Put on a smile.
You'll feel better!

A wise man restrains his anger and overlooks insults. This is to his credit.

Proverbs 19:11

Wisdom allows you
to look beyond
the present to
see the possible
consequences of
your actions.
Be a "wise guy"
or a "wise gal"
in the best sense
of the word.

…"I came naked from my mother's womb," he said, "and I shall have nothing when I die. The Lord gave me everything I had, and they were his to take away. Blessed be the name of the Lord."

Job 1:21

You work, work,
and work to
accumulate all
those things you
can't take with you
when you die!
What you can
take with you
is a holy life
and lots of love.
Work to accumulate
what counts.

Never pay back evil for evil. Do things in such a way that everyone can see you are honest clear through.

Romans 12:17

You hit me,
and I hit you.
You ruin
my reputation,
and I ruin yours.
You steal from me,
and I steal from you.
This is why families
and countries decay.
Evil must be
stopped with the
power of love.
It's your choice.

Pity me, O Lord, for I am weak. Heal me, for my body is sick, and I am upset and disturbed. My mind is filled with apprehension and gloom. Oh, restore me soon.

Psalm 6:2-3

The lower you fall,
the greater the
need to lift your
heart to the Lord.
Don't wait.
Do it now.

What a shame — yes, how stupid! — to decide before knowing the facts!

Proverbs 18:13

Are you impetuous?
Do you judge
before you know
the whole story?
Your life would
be less stressful
if you didn't
jump to conclusions.

Temptation is the pull of man's own evil thoughts and wishes. These evil thoughts lead to evil actions and afterwards to the death penalty from God.

James 1:14-15

Watch your
thought life!
Evil thoughts give
rise to evil actions.
Seek good thoughts
to give rise to
good actions.
You reap
what you sow.

Don't spend your time in wild parties and getting drunk or in adultery and lust, or fighting, or jealousy. But ask the Lord Jesus Christ to help you live as you should, and don't make plans to enjoy evil.

Romans 13:13-14

Saint Paul could
be describing
society today.
He is telling you
not to live like this.
Ask God to help you.

I keep thinking of the good old days of the past, long since ended.

Psalm 77:5

Were the good old days really that good? Surely, stress had its impact then as now. You just didn't call it "stress" because the word wasn't coined yet!

You cannot serve two masters: God and money. For you will hate one and love the other, or else the other way around.

Matthew 6:24

Do you choose
money over God?
Do you make
money your
end-all and be-all?
If so, no wonder
you are stressed!

Why was I ever born? For my life has been but trouble and sorrow and shame.

Jeremiah 20:18

You are a
reflection of God.
Shame, sorrow,
trouble do not
lessen your value
in God's eyes.
You'll always be
precious to Him.

In everything you do, stay away from complaining and arguing, so that no one can speak a word of blame against you. You are to live innocent lives as children of God in a dark world full of people who are crooked and stubborn. Shine out among them like beacon lights, holding out to them the Word of God.

Philippians 2:14-16

Have you
noticed that it
seems the news
is 90% gloom
and 10% uplifting?
Evil actions are
reported, but rarely
good deeds.
You need
good news
to lift up your spirit.
Spread cheer
to others.

Don't repay evil for evil. Wait for the Lord to handle the matter.

Proverbs 20:22

So God is just
too slow for you.
You want
instant payback!
Remember, you
may be in error.
God is a just God,
He'll take care of it,
so calm down!

And who can tell whether my son will be a wise man or a fool? And yet all I have will be given to him — how discouraging!

Ecclesiastes 2:19

Parents, don't give
up on your children.
They go through
strange phases
that are hard
to understand.
This causes you
much stress!
Place them in God's
hands every day.
God can
work miracles!

Jesus replied that people soon became thirsty again after drinking this water. "But the water I give them," he said, "becomes a perpetual spring within them, watering them forever with eternal life."

John 4:13-14

It is stressful when
you are thirsty.
It is also stressful
if you live your life
without meaning.
Thirst for God.

Stop listening to teaching that contradicts what you know is right.

Proverbs 19:27

There are false
teachers promising
you the empty
treasures of this world.
Your treasure
is in heaven.
God has given you
Christ as your map.
His way is love.

Lord, You alone can heal me, you alone can save, and my praises are for you alone.

Jeremiah 17:14

The healing arts
exist only because of
God's healing energy.
When you thank your
health professional,
do you also
remember to
thank God?
All power comes
from Him.

There is no need to fear when times of trouble come, ...I want you to trust me in your time of trouble, so I can rescue you, and you can give me glory.

Psalm 49:5, 50:15

You will always
be a child of God
even if you
live to be a
100 years old.
Shout "Save me"
and leap into
His arms.

I, yes, I alone am he who blots away your sins for my own sake and will never think of them again.

Isaiah 43:25

Stop bemoaning
any longer
your past life.
God's mercy is
greater than any sins
you have committed.
He has forgotten
them if you've
asked forgiveness.
Why don't you
do the same?

"Now my soul is deeply troubled. Shall I pray, 'Father, save me from what lies ahead?' But that is the very reason I came!"

John 12:27

Christ didn't find it
easy to suffer and
die for you.
His sweat came as
drops of blood.
Christ experienced
profound stress.
Do you see
how much
God loves you?

Glory to God in the highest heaven," they sang, "and peace on earth for all those pleasing him."

Luke 2:14

When stress is gone,
there is peace.
Peace be to you
today and always.

Alleluia!

BIBLE VERSES USED OLD TESTAMENT

Ecclesiastes	1:8, 1:15, 2:19, 8:14
Exodus	3:11-12, 4:1, 18:18
Genesis	6:5-6, 27:46
Isaiah	40:31, 42:3, 43:25
Jeremiah	17:10, 17:14, 20:18, 23:24
Job	1:21, 2:10
Numbers	11:11,14-15
Proverbs	12:25, 14:30, 15:1, 15:4, 15:17, 16:32, 17:14, 18:13, 19:11, 19:19, 19:27, 20:22, 29:11
Psalms	6:2-3, 27:1, 31:9-10, 32:3, 34:19, 37:11, 43:5, 49:5, 50:15, 77:4, 77:5, 86:1, 86:6-7, 102:1-2, 119:31, 127:2, 133:1, 142:6, 143:7

BIBLE VERSES USED NEW TESTAMENT

1 Corinthians	7:32, 10:13
2 Corinthians	4:17, 13:11
Ephesians	4:31-32
Hebrews	12:15
James	1:14-15, 1:21
John	2:24-25, 4:6, 4:13-14, 12:27, 14:1, 14:27
Luke	2:14, 3:8, 10:40-42, 11:17, 12:25, 18:4-5
Mark	1:12-13
Matthew	6:24, 23:4
1 Peter	2:1
Philippians	2:14-16, 4:6-7
Romans	12:12, 12:17, 12:18, 13:13-14, 14:13

BOOK ORDER FORM

	Per book
God Knows Best About Stress	$9.95
God Knows Best About Joy	$9.95
One-Liners from God	$9.95
Postage and Handling per book	$2.00

Send check or money order (in USA currency) made payable to the ***Sisters of Mercy***.

Mail with form to: Fun Nun Books
College of Saint Mary, 1901 S. 72nd St.
Omaha, NE USA 68124-2377

Your Name: ______________________________

Company: ______________________________

Address: ______________________________

City: ______________________ State: ________

Country: ______________ Zip: ______________

Telephone: ______________________________

Fax: ______________________________

E-Mail: ______________________________

$11.95 X ________ Book(s) = Total: ______________

THANK YOU FOR YOUR ORDER!

CASSETTE TAPE ORDER FORM

Cost per tape including postage $11

__ Laughter/Jokes/Laughter

__ Wellness and Your Funny Bone

__ The Merry Christian

__ Self-Image and Interpersonal Relationships

__ Communication and Interpersonal Relationships

__ Stress: What's It All About?

__ Relaxation Techniques

__ The Mind/Body Connection

$11 x (quantity) ________ = Total: ______________

Send check or money order
(in USA currency)
made payable to the ***Sisters of Mercy***.

Mail form with information on page 170 to:

Fun Nun
College of Saint Mary
1901 S.72 St., Omaha, NE USA, 68124-2377

THANK YOU FOR YOUR ORDER!

Please send the tapes indicated on page 169 to:

Your Name: ______________________________

Company: ______________________________

Address: ______________________________

City: ______________________________

State: ______________________________

Country: ______________________________

Zip: ______________________________

Telephone: ______________________________

Fax: ______________________________

E-mail: ______________________________

Sister Mary Christelle is a professional speaker and a member of the National Speakers Association.

Invite the FUN NUN to your next event!

Conventions

Meetings

Keynote Address

In-Service

www.FUNNUN.com

funnun@csm.edu

402-399-2474